LIGHTNING
BOLT
BOOKS ™

Meet a Baby Chicken

Buffy Silverman

Lerner Publications • Minneapolis

To my boychik
Jake. Love, Mom

Lerner Publications Company
A division of Lerner Publishing Group, Inc.
241 First Avenue North
Minneapolis, MN 55401 USA

For reading levels and more information, look up this title at www.lernerbooks.com.

Library of Congress Cataloging-in-Publication Data

Names: Silverman, Buffy, author.
Title: Meet a baby chicken / Buffy Silverman.
Description: Minneapolis : Lerner Publications, [2016] | Series: Lightning bolt books. Baby farm animals | Audience: Ages 5–8. | Audience: K to grade 3. | Includes bibliographical references and index.
Identifiers: LCCN 2015035201| ISBN 9781512408034 (lb : alk. paper) | ISBN 9781512410259 (eb pdf)
Subjects: LCSH: Chicks—Juvenile literature. | Chickens—Development—Juvenile literature.
Classification: LCC SF498.4 .S55 2016 | DDC 636.5/07—dc23

LC record available at http://lccn.loc.gov/2015035201

Manufactured in the United States of America
1 – BP – 7/15/16

Table of Contents

Breaking Out!

Peep! Peep! Peep! A baby chicken calls from inside its egg. It is getting ready to break out.

A chick begins as a single cell inside an egg. The cell divides many times as the chick grows. The egg's yolk gives food to the growing chick. After three weeks, the chick is ready to hatch.

The yellow liquid in an egg is the yolk.

The chick pecks from inside its egg. It taps with the hard bump at the end of its beak. This bump is called an egg tooth. The egg tooth cracks the shell.

The hole in the shell grows larger and larger. Finally, the chick struggles out. Its feathers are damp. Bits of shell might stick to its skin. The little chick is tired!

A mother hen stays on her nest for two days after her first egg hatches. The new chicks press under her wings. They need their mother's warmth. She broods them.

This hen keeps her chicks warm.

Chicks inside their eggs hear their mother clucking to them.

Some of the eggs have not yet hatched. The hen clucks to them. The chicks break their shells. Soon all the chicks break out.

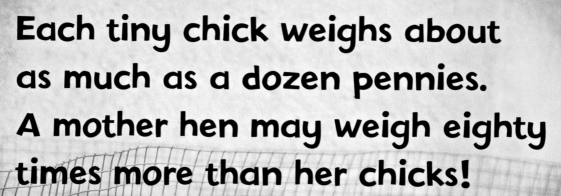

Each tiny chick weighs about
as much as a dozen pennies.
A mother hen may weigh eighty
times more than her chicks!

Mama's Shadows

A chick's feathers dry after hatching. Fluffy feathers, called down, keep chicks warm. Down can be yellow, gray, brown, black, or white.

Little chicks stand and walk soon after they hatch. They follow their mom when she leaves the nest.

Chicks stay near their mom while exploring the world.

Young chicks know the sound of their mother's clucks. They can find her in a crowded barn. They run to her when they hear a new noise.

Chicks go to their mom for protection.

The hen pecks at bits of food. She clucks at her chicks. Her clucks tell the chicks to peck too.

This chick pecks at the ground to find something to eat.

The little chicks peck at grains and seeds. They try to catch flies. They learn to eat.

The chicks watch the hen drink water. Then they practice drinking too.

These chickens drink water on a farm. Chicks learn to eat and drink by watching their mothers.

At night, the chicks snuggle under their mother's wings. They sleep after a busy day. They are warm and safe.

Chicks snuggle close to their mom before they go to sleep.

Gobbling in the Grass

At ten days old, a chick starts roaming away from the hen. The chick has learned to scratch the ground to find food. It pecks at everything it sees.

Chicks begin exploring on their own as they get older.

A chick pecks at a worm. It gobbles grubs. It eats corn, soybeans, and seeds.

This chick has found a worm to eat!

Chicks peck at one another too. Stronger chicks win their fights. A group of chicks learn which chicks and adults are the strongest. This is called a pecking order.

Over time, the chicks lose their fluffy down. They grow new feathers. They start to look like grown-up chickens!

This chick will soon be fully grown.

The young chicks peep loudly when there is danger. The mother hen still protects them. The chicks sleep under her and stay warm.

Mother chickens keep their chicks close even as they grow older.

Out of the Nest

By the time a chick is about four months old, it no longer sleeps in its mother's nest. A hen pushes her growing chicks away. They are ready to take care of themselves.

This chick is almost ready to live on its own.

The chicks take care of their new feathers. This is called preening. They fix their feathers with their beaks. They roll in the dust to clean themselves.

This chicken takes a dust bath!

By six months old, chickens grow wattles under their beaks. They also grow combs on their heads. The males grow spurs on their legs. Now the males are roosters!

Can you find this rooster's wattle, comb, and spurs?

A female chick becomes a hen. She starts to lay eggs when she is six to ten months old. A hen can lay more than five hundred eggs during her life. She can live for ten years or more.

This hen is old enough to lay eggs.

The young hens cluck. They are ready for their first chicks to hatch!

Why People Raise Chickens

Most chickens live on farms. People raise them to sell their eggs. They also raise chickens for meat. In the United States, people eat eight billion chickens a year. Some people raise chickens in their backyards and gather their eggs. Chickens can even live in cities! Chickens help gardeners by pecking weeds, eating bugs, and improving the soil. Chicken feathers can be made into paper, plastic, and even diapers.

Fun Facts

- The eggs you buy in a store cannot grow into chicks. They are not fertilized. The hen that laid them did not mate with a rooster.

- There are about twenty-five billion chickens in the world. That's almost four times as many chickens as people.

- Adult chickens can eat lizards and mice!

Glossary

brood: to warm, protect, and cover eggs and chicks with the wings or body

cell: a microscopic structure that living things are made of

comb: a fleshy part on top of a chicken's head

egg tooth: a knob at the tip of a beak that a bird or a reptile uses to break through an eggshell and hatch

spur: a sharp part of a rooster's leg that sticks out

wattle: a fleshy part that hangs down from a chicken's chin

yolk: the yellow part of an egg that nourishes a growing chick

Further Reading

Easy Science for Kids: Chickens
http://easyscienceforkids.com/all-about
-chickens

Enchanted Learning: All about Chickens
http://www.enchantedlearning.com/subjects/birds
/info/chicken.shtml

Lundgren, Julie K. *Chickens.* Vero Beach, FL:
Rourke, 2011.

Merritt, Robin. *The Life Cycle of a Chicken.*
Mankato, MN: Child's World, 2012.

Page, Robin. *A Chicken Followed Me Home!
Questions and Answers about a Familiar Fowl.*
New York: Beach Lane Books, 2015.

Index

Photo Acknowledgments

The images in this book are used with the permission of: © Robynrg/Shutterstock.com, p. 2; © Karen Jackson/flickr.com (CC BY-ND 2.0); © Hans D Dossenbach/ardea.com /Pantheon/SuperStock, p. 5; © Fabio Colombini Medeiros/Animals Animals, p. 6; © Photowitch/Dreamstime.com, p. 7; © Robert Maier/Animals Animals, p. 8; © Thierry Vialard/Dreamstime.com, p. 9; © Catalina Zaharescu Tiensuu/Dreamstime.com, p. 10; © Perutskyi Petro/Shutterstock.com, p. 11; © Judith Dzierzawa/Dreamstime.com, p. 12; © KAMONRAT/Shutterstock.com, p. 13; © Alexandru Ionas-salagean/Dreamstime.com, p. 14; © iStockphoto.com/Madzia71, p. 15; © iStockphoto.com/simbon4o, p. 16; © iStockphoto.com/malerapaso, p. 17; © sevenke/Shutterstock.com, p. 18; © iStockphoto.com/eurobanks, p. 19; © Jorja M. Vornheder/Moment Open/Getty Images, p. 20; © Schubbel/Shutterstock.com, p. 21; © Epitavi/Shutterstock.com, p. 22; © Marcel Berendsen/Dreamstime.com, p. 23; © Chaiyabutra/Shutterstock.com, p. 24; © Tanor/Shutterstock.com, p. 25; © Lightpoet/Dreamstime.com, p. 26; © Laurenchristinethorpe/Dreamstime.com, p. 27; © iStockphoto.com/Vassiliy Vishnevskiy, p. 29; © iStockphoto.com/vuk8691, p. 30.

Front cover: © catalinr/Shutterstock.com.

Main body text set in Johann Light 30/36.